The Horse Thieves, 1901, Charles Russell. Plains Indians regarded horse stealing as a brave act and an alternate, bloodless means to making war on enemy tribes. (Courtesy, Amon Carter Museum of Western Art, Fort Worth)

THE GREAT AMERICAN WEST

Home Library Publishing Company
Fort Atkinson, Wisconsin

Breaking a Pony, or Fording a Stream, 1905, Henry F. Farny.
One of the gentler Indian methods of breaking a horse was to lead it into water,
which would hinder and tire the horse while it became accustomed
to a rider and halter. (Thomas Gilcrease Institute
of American History and Art, Tulsa)

Turf House on the Plains, n.d., Karl Wimar.
Lacking wood and bricks, plainsmen constructed shelters
from such readily available materials as sod and grass.
(Bancroft Library, University of California, Berkeley)

CONTENTS

Introduction 4

I Trail to the Setting Sun 6

II Images of a Promised Land 16

III The Native American: Ceremonies and War Cries 28

IV Men of the Horse 54

V A Bloody Heritage 66

VI Of Legendary Men 86

Index of Artists 96

Introduction

"Go West, young man," said Horace Greeley, a confirmed Easterner, and thousands did, but that was already halfway through the nineteenth century. The westering drive that brought Europeans and especially the people from the British Isles into the coastal lands that were to become the original thirteen United States began a good two centuries earlier at Plymouth, Massachusetts, and Jamestown, Virginia. A century before those two settlements, Cortez undertook the still astonishing conquest of Mexico, an event which, although outside the United States, was to have profound, decisive effects on the nature of the life that eventually came into being in our Western states.

The keenest appreciation of the West by those who remain in or return to the East goes back before Greeley. The key saying, almost the charter, of the whole westering enterprise was written by Bishop Berkeley, the philosopher, who tried to found a school for American Indians and failed, but who did spend three or four years as far west from Britain as Newport, Rhode Island, almost half a century before the American Revolution. His poem was called, in the manner of his day, "On the Prospect of Planting Arts and Learning in America," and in it he wrote the immortal line: "Westward the course of empire takes its way."

For Bishop Berkeley, Newport was already about as far West as one would care to go. He knew, of course, that there were lands beyond the Appalachians, but the very shore of the New World was already the mystical West with its promise, at once encouraging and discouraging. Soon, however, the first "West," that is, the Atlantic shore of the New World, was inhabited, and prosperous or hardy settlers were looking to the interior — the Ohio valley and over the Appalachians — to newer frontiers. After the settlement of the Northwest Territory and the explorations of Lewis and Clark (1803-1806), the vast open spaces of the Trans-Mississippi West then beckoned early white migrators. Trappers, explorers, soldiers and gold prospectors were followed by artists who recorded on canvas their experiences in the new land.

Encampment on the Plains, n.d., Worthington Whittredge.
(Joslyn Art Museum, Northern Natural Gas Collection, Omaha)

The Herd, 1899, Frank Reaugh. (Thomas Gilcrease Institute of American History and Art, Tulsa)

The single, outstanding, new and original form of art that America brought into existence was Western painting and sculpture, for the very good reason that the way of life shown in Western art had never existed anywhere else. In the following pages is a history of the adventure of the American West as it was discovered over and over again by painters, sketchers and sculptors. These artists, in turn, had a great influence on how the rest of America (and the world) came to regard the land and the inhabitants of the West.

The art of the West begins with the Indians. Although white artists did not seriously borrow from Indian art until the mid-twentieth century, the American Indian was the subject of Western art from the outset. No one made a more serious and utterly dedicated record of the native people than George Catlin, the first outstanding painter of the Plains frontier. Catlin's aspiration was to preserve the brilliance of the Indian from the black and blue cloak of civilization, which was destined, he said, to obliterate nature's beauty. No other artist was so accepted by the Plains Indians, with whom he lived for six years.

Other superb artists who portrayed the West included Karl Bodmer, a cool, but skilled observer of Indian customs; Alfred Jacob Miller, a young romantic whose paintings gave the West a holiday look; Seth Eastman, a military man who fought and lived with many Indian tribes; George Caleb Bingham, the Missouri-bred painter of mellow river scenes of life balanced between frontier and civilization; and Albert Bierstadt, promoter par excellence of the grandeur of the Western landscape.

Western art chronicles a great period and the classic struggle in the history of America — that of the Anglo-Americans against the Indians, against sheer space, against assorted foreign goverments with claims on part of the American territory, against one another and, finally, against the weakness within. The results have been varied, but there is no question that the West ranks with the Civil War — in some ways outranks it — as the epic place, the epic events, the epic people, of the United States.

I Trail to the Setting Sun

By the 1820's, after George Rogers Clark had secured the Old Northwest for the United States, the true frontier had moved west of the Mississippi. First the mountain men, other trappers and explorers, then the gold miners, missionaries and wagon trains of pioneers seemed determined to fulfill the romantic prophecy that "Westward the course of empire takes its way."

Westward the Course of Empire Takes its Way, n.d.,
Emanuel Leutze. Leutze's painting symbolizes the westering enterprise
that began with the discovery of the New World. Hailing the land beyond
the mountain walls are pioneer families leading their wagon trains
in anticipation of settling the West. (Photo by George F. Mobley,
Courtesy U.S. Capitol Historical Society)

Opening the way West
for all who came after . . .

Opposite: **George Rogers Clark on His Way to Kaskaskia**, n.d., Howard Pyle. While Clark stands guard against British and Indian enemies, his band crosses the Ohio River. Because of his military victories, the Northwest Territory was granted to the new American nation in 1783, opening the way West for all who came after. (Thomas Gilcrease Institute of American History and Art, Tulsa)

The Trapper's Return, 1851, George Caleb Bingham. Inner North America was first penetrated by French fur trappers and traders in search of beaver pelts. They used the riverways for transportation. (The Detroit Institute of Arts, gift of Dexter M. Ferry, Jr.)

Blazing their trails
into the heartland of the frontier West . . .

Noon-day Rest, n.d., Alfred Jacob Miller. Fur trappers acted as trail blazers by exploring farther westward in their search for valuable animal skins. (Walters Art Gallery, Baltimore)

Opposite: **Trappers Starting for the Beaver Hunt**, n.d., Alfred Jacob Miller. Mountain men, trappers who stayed in the mountains most of the year, wore buckskin clothes and caps of skins for protection from the elements. A bullet pouch and powder horn commonly were slung over the shoulder. (Walters Art Gallery, Baltimore)

The new, emergent American West . . .

The Scouting Party, 1851,
William Ranney. After the Civil War,
the West no longer was the domain
of the solitary trapper and explorer
for then came the proto-cowboys, scouting
the vast land for its cattle raising
and homesteading potentials.
(National Cowboy Hall of Fame
and Western Heritage Center,
Oklahoma City)

12

The daring men and women
who carved an empire out of the wilderness . . .

Opposite: **Caravan en Route**, ca. 1859, Alfred Jacob
Miller. In this rendering of an actual expedition, the travelers
were depicted as a great horde that seemingly filled the plain,
though in reality they numbered about 100 men.
(Walters Art Gallery, Baltimore)

Crossing the Kansas, ca. 1859, Alfred Jacob Miller.
Crossing rivers posed a serious threat to the safety of a westward-bound expedition.
According to the artist who accompanied this caravan, despite the danger, there
was "a great deal of fun and merriment intermingled with hard swearing
in several languages." (Walters Art Gallery, Baltimore)

The Voyageurs,
1846, Charles Deas.
Canoers transported
goods in the Great
Lakes region.
(Museum of Fine Arts,
Boston, M. and M.
Karolik Collection)

Moonlight View on the Mississippi, 75 Miles Above St. Louis,
ca. 1847-49, Seth Eastman. Under the fantastic moonlit patterns in the sky,
a vignette of natural violence — Indian hunting deer — blends with
the overall untamed scene. (The St. Louis Art Museum, purchase
funds donated by Mr. and Mrs. Warren Shapleigh,
Mr. and Mrs. Gordon Hertslet, Mr. William
Pagenstecker, and the Garden Club of St. Louis)

II Images of a Promised Land

Nothing in Eastern America prepared those migrating west for
the vastness, harshness and majestic grandeur of the Far West. The
great herds of buffalo wandering across endless plains, the broad,
beautiful rivers and turbulent streams, the rugged canyons and
towering mountains — these struck newcomers with such an impact
— both real and mystical — that these vistas became a pervasive and
dominant part of America's rich natural heritage.

The Buffalo Trail, 1867-68, Albert Bierstadt.
Though at first glance this has the elements of an Eastern scene,
the reality of the towering trees, the giant herds of bison and the wide river
confront the viewer with the vast spaces of the American West.
Bierstadt's landscape painting did much to acquaint the public
with the richness of the American land and helped popularize
the West in the East. (Museum of Fine Arts,
Boston, M. and M. Karolik Collection)

17

Finding in mountains some special contact with divinity...

Above: **View in the Big Bend of the Upper Missouri**, 1832,
George Catlin. From 1830 to 1836 Catlin roamed the Western territories,
painting in the open air rather than finishing a canvas in the artificial
confines of a studio. (Courtesy, National Collection of Fine Arts,
Smithsonian Institution) Opposite, below: **Valmont Valley, Colorado**,
1870-75, Worthington Whittredge. A distant settlement is dwarfed
by the horizontal band of mountains, the bright light
and the empty space of the West. (Courtesy, Mr. and Mrs.
Jonathan C. Calvert, San Antonio)

Western Landscape, 1868, Albert Bierstadt.
(Steven Straw Company, Seabrook, New Hampshire)

**The landscape of the West —
an overwhelming feeling
of nature's majesty and beauty . . .**

Grand Canyon, 1913,
Thomas Moran. Moran painted this view
of the canyon after forty years' familiarity with
the area's fantastic natural attractions. His paintings
helped the public see the need for wilderness
preservation which culminated in our National
Parks system. (Thomas Gilcrease Institute
of American History and Art, Tulsa)

The destiny and the dream of innocence and nature . . .

In the Rocky Mountains, n.d., Alfred Jacob Miller.
A record of daily camp life is this scene with Captain Stewart
inspecting his camp, a rather unusual painting in that human efforts
supersede the background majesty. (Joslyn Art Museum, Omaha)

Right: **Giant Redwoods of California**, n.d., Albert Bierstadt. (Courtesy, Bershire Museum) Below: **California Pines**, 1878, William Keith. Keith often made sketching trips along the California coast, at times with the naturalist, John Muir, and faithfully recorded the look of the land. (Los Angeles County Museum of Art, gift of Museum Patrons Association)

Lake Tahoe, California, 1867, Albert Bierstadt.
Variations of light as it plays over the landscape and sky.
Space, although vast, is shaped by distant mountains,
flat water and floating clouds. (Museum of Fine Arts,
Boston, M.and M. Karolik Collection)

A glorious vision of the most spectacular aspects of the American landscape before its erosion by humanity . . .

Mount Baker, Washington, 1869, William Keith.
As a young member of the San Francisco art community,
Keith traveled widely along the West Coast, gaining exposure to the rugged
and wild landscape. (E. B. Crocker Art Gallery, Sacramento)

The Teton Range, Idaho, 1899, Thomas Moran.
Moran was master of painting mountains. At a time when
the look of the West was unfamiliar to the majority of Americans,
he captured his vision of the glorious country and shared it
with the world. (Kimball Art Foundation, Fort Worth)

III The Native American: Ceremonies and War Cries

The native Americans, called Indians by the white man, who lived in the land that became the United States were generally hunting cultures and can accurately be described as constituting a Stone Age culture.

The great central group of tribes, the Plains Indians, were able to preserve their independence longest against the white man's encroachments, and they were by far the most important group in the history of the West. These were the nomadic and seminomadic Indians who hunted the buffalo, attacked the wagon trains, who fought the United States Cavalry and often — as at the Little Big Horn — outfought them. These were the Indians of the war path, war dance and war paint. They also made the most effective use of two gifts from the whites, the rifle and the horse.

Prairie Indian Encampment, n.d., John Mix Stanley.
A close-up of a village shows a crowd of tepees — structures made by stretching hides over wooden poles. Buffalo hides are drying in the left background. (The Detroit Institute of Arts, gift of Mrs. Blanche Ferry Hooker)

A Bird's-Eye View of the Mandan Village, 1832, George Catlin.
Catlin devoted himself unstintingly towards a faithful rendering
of the American West and particularly the American Indian. His affection
for the Indian subjects and their way of life is clear in this intimate view
of a Mandan village settled among peaceful green hills of North Dakota.
(Courtesy, National Collection of Fine Arts, Smithsonian Institution)

The Indian was the native — who could be both noble and treacherous . . .

Marriage Custom of the Indians, ca. 1850-55, Seth Eastman.
In traveling around the West, Eastman sought accurate representations
of the Indians and some of their customs.
(James Jerome Hill Reference Library, St. Paul)

Opposite: **A Blackfoot Indian**, 1888, Frederic Remington.
Living in the northwest corner of the Plains, the Blackfoot tribes
were grassland people dressing in buffalo and deerskins,
owning many horses and riding them with great skill.
(Kimbell Art Foundation, Fort Worth)

The buffalos' charging hoofbeats matched the roar of the summer thunderstorm and the winter blizzard . . .

Buffalo Hunt Under the Wolf-Skin Mask, ca. 1830, George Catlin. Warriors disguised themselves under wolf skins in order both to surprise the buffalo and to prepare themselves symbolically with wolflike stealth, courage, speed and accuracy in the hunt. (Courtesy, National Collection of Fine Arts, Smithsonian Institution)

Buffalo Hunt on Snowshoes, n.d., George Catlin. Long before
the white man's invasion, the Indians hunted buffalo without guns or horses.
Once populating the Great Plains in seemingly limitless numbers,
by 1900 some fifty million buffalo had been killed by whites,
endangering not only the species but the Indians who relied
on them for life's basics. (Thomas Gilcrease
Institute of American History and Art, Tulsa)

Sioux Indians Pursuing a Stag in Their Canoes, 1836, George Catlin. The large, triangular forms of Catlin's composition — also the form of an arrow — point off to the right, to where the stag is fleeing, to the infinity and freedom, perhaps, of the West. (Courtesy, National Collection of Fine Arts, Smithsonian Insitution)

The stag flees
to the infinity and freedom
of the West . . .

**Tis-se-woo-ha-tis, She Who Bathes
Her Knees, Wife of a Cheyenne Chief,**
1834, George Catlin. (Courtesy,
National Collection of Fine Arts,
Smithsonian Institution)

Indians in Council, ca. 1851, Seth Eastman. Basic to Indian government was the community meeting, or powwow, to discuss serious matters. Speaking would be interspersed with praying, dancing and singing until a decision on a course of action was made. (James Jerome Hill Reference Library, St. Paul)

Pride in their heritage, pride in their language, their dances and ceremonies . . .

Sioux Bear Dance, 1847, George Catlin. Catlin's paintings
of Indian dances are wonderfully strange. He emphasized what he felt
was the key to their character — mystery and supernaturalism.
(Thomas Gilcrease Institute of American History and Art, Tulsa)

Grant that we
may face the winds
and walk the good road
to the day of quiet . . .

The Bull Dance, Mandan O-kee-pa,
n.d., George Catlin. The entire
Mandan village witnessed the
elaborate ceremony, performed
to bring the buffalo herds within range.
(Courtesy, National Collection of Fine
Arts, Smithsonian Institution)

A collision of worlds that tainted Indian life . . .

Above: **Black Knife, an Apache Chief**, 1846, John Mix Stanley.
Unlike earlier Indian portraits, the artist's portrayal of Black Knife
is unposed — his subject is active and prepared for battle. (Courtesy,
National Collection of Fine Arts, Smithsonian Institution) Opposite:
Pigeon's Egg Head, 1832, George Catlin. Pigeon's Egg Head,
the son of an Assiniboin chief, is posed in a double portrait,
showing him before and after being corrupted by
the white man. (Courtesy, National Collection
of Fine Arts, Smithsonian Institution)

41

Indian Encampment in the Rockies, n.d., Albert Bierstadt.
The Rocky Mountain landscape and the Indian way of life was a foreign scene
to most Americans in 1863 when this grandiose painting was first exhibited.
(Courtesy, Whitney Gallery of Western Art, Cody, Wyoming)

Scene at Rendezvous, n.d., Alfred Jacob Miller. Indians gather
to watch the annual rendezvous of fur trappers. Once each summer
the trappers converged on an agreed-upon spot to trade their year's catch
for new supplies. (Walters Art Gallery, Baltimore)

The Great Spirit has made us all;
but he has made a great difference
between his white and red children . . .

Dakota Woman and Assiniboin Girl,
1841, Karl Bodmer. (Joslyn Art Museum,
Northern Natural Gas Company
Collection, Omaha)

These were the Indians of the war path, the war dance and the war paint . . .

Beating a Retreat, 1842, Alfred Jacob Miller.
Warriors attacking each other on the Plains became a conventional
impression, among whites, of Indian life. (Museum of Fine
Arts, Boston, M. and M. Karolik Collection)

Right: **Pehriska-Ruhpa, Moennitarri Warrior, in the costume of the Dog Danse**, 1841, Karl Bodmer. The artist's details of anatomy and costume are precise. (Joslyn Art Museum, Northern Natural Gas Collection, Omaha) Below: **Indian Warfare**, 1908, Frederic Remington. Remington, the master painter of the horse, shows the magnificent Indian horsemanship. (Thomas Gilcrease Institute of American History and Art, Tulsa)

47

A nation of human beings whose origin
is beyond the reach of human investigation . . .

Above: **Pawnee Indians Watching the Caravan**, 1837,
Alfred Jacob Miller. (Walters Art Gallery, Baltimore)

Right: **Arapahos**, n.d., Alfred Jacob Miller. The
Arapahos were a meticulously ceremonious people
who were generally tolerant of the white man.
(Walters Art Gallery, Baltimore)

In the Enemy's Country, 1900, Henry F. Farny. Tense and wary of attack
in a dry, gritty land, this scene presents the Indian's point of view in the eternal struggle
with the white man. (Mr. W. J. Williams, Cincinnati)

The Indians' misfortune has consisted chiefly in our ignorance of their true native character and disposition . . .

The Two Crows, after 1850, George Catlin. (Courtesy, The Newberry Library, Ayer Collection)

The Buffalo Hunt, 1860, Karl Wimar. The Indians' skill
at hunting buffalo with bow and arrow, spear and gun is depicted here
as their larger-than-life bodies seem to overpower completely
both their horses and their quarry. (Collection,
Washington University Gallery of Art, St. Louis)

**Artists were recording and preserving
the Indian's way of life in the certain knowledge that
that life was already in sight of its end . . .**

Opposite, above: **Indian Camp at Dawn**, n.d., Jules Tavernier.
Before the white man arrived, Indians appeared to have had all the time and space
in the world. (Thomas Gilcrease Institute of American History and Art, Tulsa)
Below: **Pawnee Indians Migrating**, ca. 1859, Alfred Jacob Miller.
As the white man advanced farther West, he forced thousands of Indians
to resettle in new lands. (Walters Art Gallery, Baltimore)

IV Men of the Horse

The heyday of open-range cattle empires and of the cowboy, whose efforts and accomplishments made them possible, began after 1865 and lasted hardly a generation. The cowboy was a nimble and gritty, overworked laborer who rode endless, lonely miles in the rain, wind and dust to guide and protect the longhorns; his skills in working with horses and the cattle were essential to doing his job. As the decades passed he became America's most enduring hero of its boldest legend. He was transformed into a model of courage, pride and independence, a fierce competitor who was slow to speak but quick to defend his life and his freedom against all comers, an American ideal.

Hunting Wild Horses, 1846, William Ranney. Ranney documented the Mexican influence on later American cowboy dress and gear. The shape of the saddle was handed down virtually unchanged, while the boot would later be shortened to mid-calf. (Joslyn Art Museum, Northern Natural Gas Company Collection, Omaha)

Stampeded by Lightning, 1908, Frederic Remington. Expert riding
was a necessary skill for the cowboy who drove cattle from the range to the railhead
for shipment. To slow the nighttime stampede of frightened longhorns,
he rides to head-off the lead animals. (Thomas Gilcrease
Institute of American History and Art, Tulsa)

Above: **Roping Wild Horses,** 1877, James Walker. (Thomas Gilcrease Institute of American History and Art, Tulsa) Right: **Vacqueros Roping Horses in a Corral,** 1877, James Walker. Walker shows with great detail the refinements of technique and equipment which the Mexican *vacqueros* of California passed on to their American counterparts, the cowboys. While the fancy decorations on pants and jackets and the cut of the hat would be altered, the *vacqueros'* skill with horses and ropes would be passed down intact. (Thomas Gilcrease Institute of American History and Art, Tulsa)

dusty lives with a certain posturing pride . . .

Left: **Arizona Cowboy**, 1901, Frederic Remington. The later-day cowboy wore broad, leather chaps, a kerchief and a hip holster. (Rockwell Gallery, Corning, New York) Below: **Californianos at the Horse Roundup**, n.d., James Walker. Mexican ancestors to the cowboy worked with lariats, a hooped and knotted piece of rope, when rounding up wild mustangs. (Photo courtesy of Patricia Hills, Curator, Whitney Museum of American Art)

The relationship between man and horse
was a practical arrangement . . .

Halt on the Prairie, n.d., William Ranney. As the frontier moved
from the Mississippi plains to the Southwest, Texan-style habits — such as
the cut of the hat and the use of horses for transportation
rather than as pack animals — gained wider acceptance.
(Courtesy, Mr. C. R. Smith, Washington, D.C.)

The ability to endure was fundamental to a cowboy's survival . . .

Bronc in Cow Camp, 1897, Charles Russell.
As a well-known chronicler of the cowboy's daily life,
Russell captured the havoc and humor caused by a bronc's disruption
of the range hands' breakfast. (Courtesy, Amon Carter
Museum of Western Art, Fort Worth)

The Roundup, 1913, Charles Russell.
(Montana Historical Society, McKay Collection)

Jerked Down, 1907, Charles Russell. The skill of cowboys at work is authentically detailed in this painting of unexpected trouble when a steer becomes entangled in a line. The heyday of cowboys came after 1865 when millions of cattle were herded, and ended about 1890, by which time most of the open range was fenced in. (Thomas Gilcrease Institute of American History and Art, Tulsa)

A man slow-spoken but as proud as an eagle and as ready for a fight as a bobcat . . .

Calling the Horses (Get Your Ropes), 1899, Charles Russell.
"Get your ropes" was the nightherder's morning call to wake
the cow camp, which is shown in various stages of readiness
for the day's work. In the distance, a cloud of dust indicates
that part of the herd is on the loose and needs to be
rounded up. (Kimball Art Foundation, Fort Worth)

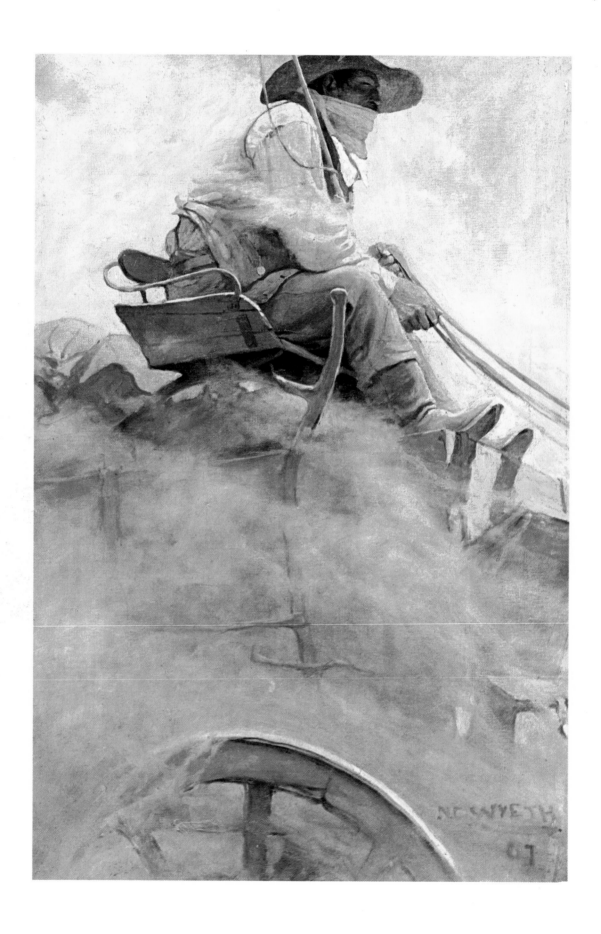

Hard-riding, fast-shooting hombres . . .

Enter the Law, 1924, E. C. Ward. Kicking up dust as he canters past two relaxed onlookers, the grizzled, steely-eyed sheriff arrives in town and creates a sense of impending confrontation. (Thomas Gilcrease Institute of American History and Art, Tulsa)

Opposite: **The Ore Wagon**, 1908, Newell Convers Wyeth. With his kerchief pulled over his mouth to keep from choking on the ever-present dust, a driver handles the reins that control the horses pulling his wagon. (Courtesy, Southern Arizona Bank and Trust Company, Tucson)

v A Bloody Heritage

An essential part of the story of America's West is violence — altercations, shootouts, skirmishes, massacres and wars between soldiers and warriors, between one Indian nation and another, between cowboys and townfolk, between outlaws and posses, between men and beasts. It was because of this violence that it became known as the Wild West.

Attack On the Wagon Train, 1904, Charles Russell. Wagons loaded with goods on an overland trek risked ambushes by Indians. The horse in the foreground has the mark of honor for having participated in raids against enemy Indian tribes. (Thomas Gilcrease Institute of American History and Art, Tulsa)

The Death of Jane McCrea, 1804, John Vanderlyn. Though the
actual story of Jane McCrea's tragic death is shrouded in mystery, the artist portrays
her Indian murderers to be savage and uncontrolled.
(Wadsworth Atheneum, Hartford, Connecticut)

The Attack on an Emigrant Train, 1856, Karl Wimar. After the 1848 discovery of gold in California, caravans of prospectors took to the trails. They faced the same dangers as other wagon trains: disease, harsh weather, wagon breakdowns and attacks from hostile Indians. (University of Michigan Museum of Art, bequest of Henry C. Lewis)

In the relationships between settlers and Indians,
often the only law was that of vengeance . . .

When Sioux and Blackfeet Meet, 1903, Charles Russell.
(Thomas Gilcrease Institute of American History and Art, Tulsa)

70

Hardy men from two cultures faced each other across a great chasm of history and spirit . . .

Opposite: **The Death Struggle,** 1845, Charles Deas. A mounted trapper engages in a knife-slashing, cliff-hanging struggle with his Indian enemy. (Shelburne Museum, Shelburne, Vermont) Above: **Immigrants,** 1904, Frederic Remington. The Indians choose a strategic moment to attack a wagon train — when the lead wagon has just started to ford a stream and the driver has only his long prod for defense. (The Museum of Fine Arts, Houston, The Hogg Brothers Collection)

Cavalry Charge Across the Southern Plains, 1907, Frederic Remington.
This charge shows the U.S. Cavalry in wholly coordinated, disciplined advance.
Their pistols are cocked and held aloft until they get closer to their target.
(The Metropolitan Museum of Art, gift of several gentlemen)

Like the infantry's quality of taking
and holding ground, so the cavalry's coherence
contributed mightily to the winning of the West . . .

Breaking Through the Lines, n.d., Charles Schreyvogel.
Authenticity and dramatic action are hallmarks of Schreyvogel's cavalry scenes.
This one could hold its own with even the most lively Western movie.
(Thomas Gilcrease Institute of American History and Art, Tulsa)

The legendary Old West confrontations of films and fiction have been depicted more authentically in art . . .

Above: **The Last March,** 1906, Frederic Remington. (Remington Art Museum, Ogdensburg, New York) Left: **The Fight for the Water Hole,** 1901, Frederic Remington. The artist shows an area of cowboy-Indian animosity seldom depicted in popular literature, movies or television. Scarcity of life-sustaining water caused truly life or death struggles. (The Museum of Fine Arts, Houston, The Hogg Brothers Collection)

The Duel: Tomahawk and Sabre, 1902, Charles Schreyvogel. Men of two
cultures battle using two different weapons indicative of their distinct heritages.
(Thomas Gilcrease Institute of American History and Art, Tulsa)

The litter of corpses and wounded touches us with the grim reality of the wars on the Plains . . .

The Battle of War Bonnet Creek, n.d., Frederic Remington.
In 1876 in the extreme northwestern corner of Nebraska the cavalry fought with the Cheyenne and Sioux Indians. The Indians were defeated and driven back to their reservations. (Thomas Gilcrease Institute of American History and Art, Tulsa)

Encounters between man
and wild animals of the wilderness...

Above: **Buffalo Hunt,** n.d., Walter Shirlaw. Trying for an immediate kill,
an Indian aims his spear for the buffalo's vulnerable spot at the base of the skull.
A buffalo who was merely wounded was dangerous because it would fight to the death
by thrusting its horns or trampling hunters. (Mr. C.R. Smith, Washington, D.C.)
Opposite: **Shooting a Cougar,** ca. 1859, Alfred Jacob Miller. Man and beast meet
in a deadly duel. A cougar leaps to attack the rider as he reins in his horse
to steady his aim and fires. (Walters Art Gallery, Baltimore)

To find in this harshness
the sources of the Western legend . . .

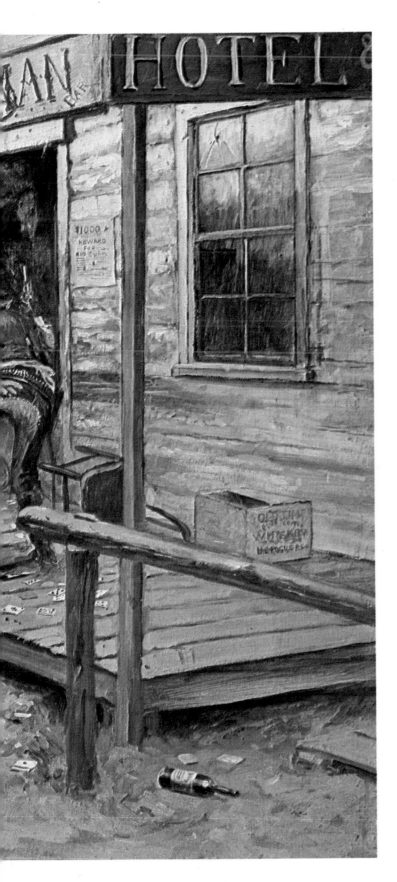

In Without Knocking, 1909,
Charles Russell. At a moment
like this of carefree hell-raising,
the remarkable command the cowboys
exercised over their horses is even
more evident than in pictures
of them at work. (Courtesy, Amon Carter
Museum of Western Art, Fort Worth)

So the gunmen shone like angry comets above
the mesa, the shabby towns and the bleak mountains ...

When Guns Speak, Death Settles Disputes, n.d., Charles Russell.
A barroom altercation makes as dramatic a subject in a painting as in a Western
movie. Gunshots were not unusual night sounds in the streets of cow towns.
Here, card players shoot it out under a starry sky. (Thomas
Gilcrease Institute of American History and Art, Tulsa)

Fleeing Bandit, n.d., William Robinson Leigh.
An outlaw flees along the wall of a canyon. He turns in the saddle
to take a shot at his pursuers, at the same time keeping the reins loose
to encourage his horse to race on. (Paine Art Center and
Arboretum, Oshkosh, Wisconsin, gift of Nathan Paine)

The hero of his country's boldest legend . . .

The Posse, 1895, Charles Russell. Legally authorized posses were often sent
in pursuit of horse thieves who were common in border states where sanctuary
in Canada was a tempting inducement to steal horses and ride to safety.
(Courtesy, Amon Carter Museum of Western Art, Fort Worth)

Opposite: **Vigilante Ways,**n.d., Olaf Carl Seltzer. "Necktie parties"
of organized citizens sometimes proved to be effective in dealing
with lawless characters until official agencies could be strengthened.
Occasionally, however, they were responsible for killing suspects
who were in fact innocent. (Thomas Gilcrease Institute
of American History and Art, Tulsa)

VI Of Legendary Men

The James Gang — Custer's Last Stand —
Kit Carson — Buffalo Bill — Wild Bill Hickok
— Lewis and Clark — these are the legends
about men who were larger than life which the
Old West gave us. Because they have been im-
mortalized the West lives on, however elusive
the true story may be.

The James Gang, n.d., Newell Convers Wyeth.
The James Brothers, Jesse and Frank, notorious bank robbers,
kept several branches of law officers in pursuit for sixteen years.
Finally, one of Jesse's men killed him, and Frank surrendered soon after.
Opposite: **Portrait of Frank Hamilton Cushing,** 1895, Thomas Eakins.
Cushing was a brilliant anthropologist, one of the founders of the
modern science through his study of the southwestern Zuñi Indian.
(Thomas Gilcrease Institute of American History and Art, Tulsa)

**In total defeat and death, they achieved
an immortality that even the most dramatic victory
could not have won them ...**

The Last Stand, Jan. 10, 1891, *Harper's Monthly*, Frederic Remington.
At the battle of Little Big Horn (Montana) in June 1876, several thousand Sioux
and Cheyenne warriors under Chief Sitting Bull killed Lieutenant Colonel George Custer
and his several hundred men. Despite controversy over Custer's true character,
he became a hero to many white Americans. (Library of Congress)

Opposite: **End of the Trail**, 1915, James Earle Fraser.
Seneca Chief Johnny Big Tree who modeled for this famous bronze sculpture
was also the model for the Indian Head nickel, or Buffalo nickel, which
James Earle Fraser made for the Federal Government.
(Brookgreen Gardens, Murrells Inlet, South Carolina)

The whole vanishing way of life
that shaped forever some part of the American soul . . .

Carson's Men, 1913, Charles Russell. Christopher "Kit" Carson
was a professional trapper, hunter and guide in the Rocky Mountain region
and later was commissioned by the government to keep peace between
the settlers and Apaches along the Santa Fe Trail (New Mexico).
Accounts of his exploits have been glorified to suit fancy
rather than fact. (Thomas Gilcrease Institute
of American History and Art, Tulsa)

Buffalo Bill on Charlie, n.d., William de la Montagne Cary.
Scout, buffalo hunter and fighter, Buffalo Bill Cody probably invented
a good deal of his own legend. He made his greatest contribution to the lore
and the love of the West by organizing, in 1887, the first Wild West Show
featuring feats of marksmanship, roping and riding and bringing these
highlights of the American West to the East Coast and to Europe.
(Thomas Gilcrease Institute of American History and Art, Tulsa)

Wild Bill Hickok, 1874, Henry H. Cross. Gaining a reputation
as one of the greatest peace officers of the West, James Butler "Wild Bill"
Hickok kept the wild cow towns under control with his skillful and willing use
of the .44 revolver. He finally paid his dues for living by the gun when
he was shot from behind in a Deadwood (Dakota Territory) saloon.
(Thomas Gilcrease Institute of American History and Art, Tulsa)

The West lives on — elusive as the shadows
on its mountainsides and the starlight in its valleys,
but eternal as the wind over its prairies . . .

Lewis and Clark at the Great Falls of the Missouri, n.d.,
Olaf Carl Seltzer. After the Louisiana Purchase of 1803 in which over
800,000 square miles of land, most of it west of the Mississippi,
was taken over, President Jefferson appointed Meriwether Lewis
and William Clark to lead an expedition. (Thomas Gilcrease
Institute of American History and Art, Tulsa)

Overleaf: **Lewis and Clark on the Lower Columbia**, 1905,
Charles Russell. Aided by their Indian woman guide, Sacajawea,
Lewis and Clark have a friendly confrontation with some Chinook Indians.
(Amon Carter Museum of Western Art, Fort Worth)